LIGHTNING
FALLS
IN LOVE

Also by Laura Kasischke

LIGHTNING
FALLS
IN LOVE

LAURA
KASISCHKE

COPPER CANYON PRESS

PORT TOWNSEND, WASHINGTON

Cover art: Walter Richard Sickert, *Summer Lightning,* National Museums Liverpool

Copper Canyon Press is in residence at Fort Worden State Park in Port Townsend, Washington, under the auspices of Centrum. Centrum is a gathering place for artists and creative thinkers from around the world, students of all ages and backgrounds, and audiences seeking extraordinary cultural enrichment.

Library of Congress Cataloging-in-Publication Data

Names: Kasischke, Laura, 1961– author.
Title: Lightning falls in love / Laura Kasischke.
Description: Port Townsend, Washington : Copper Canyon Press, [2021] |
  Summary: "In her twelfth poetry collection, Laura Kasischke makes magic with a complex alchemy of nostalgia and fire, birdwing and sorrow. Kasischke has found an entirely new way to spin beauty and pull breath from that which must be dredged up and revived before it can be left behind"— Provided by publisher.
Identifiers: LCCN 2021025527 | ISBN 9781556596360 (paperback)
Subjects: LCGFT: Poetry.
Classification: LCC PS3561.A6993 L543 2021 | DDC 811/.54—dc23
LC record available at https://lccn.loc.gov/2021025527

COPPER CANYON PRESS

Post Office Box 271
Port Townsend, Washington 98368
www.coppercanyonpress.org

for Bill

It appears she was struck by lightning—except the weather is perfectly clear with not a cloud in sight.

Patricia Cornwell

Ladybug, ladybug
Fly away home
Your house is on fire
Your children are gone.

...

Ladybug, ladybug
Fly away home
Your house is on fire
Your children have burned.

...

Ladybug, ladybug
Fly away home
Your house is on fire
Your children will burn.

...

Ladybug, ladybug
Fly away home
Your house is on fire
Your children have flown.

(common variations on nursery rhyme)

CONTENTS

LIGHTNING
FALLS
IN LOVE

The vine

This is a portrait of the tyrant as a child, smiling
shyly. It's
twilight in the vineyard, and the red night
rises from a troubled woman's
glass of wine.

It's that
tangled vine.
Always, something that whispered and flickered inside him.
We could hear it, but we tried
not to listen.

I was a child, too, then.
A girl. The flower girl. I carried
a basketful of petals—fingertips peeled from roses—and some
slippery pink ribbons

down an aisle. I was dressed
like a child
bride, or a childish lie, while the real bride waited at the altar—
smiling, honestly, while

someone raised a camera to capture us both in a moment, in
which we continue to exist
as we were then.

She's in love.
I move slowly.
The features
of her face have been erased
by sudden brightness—although
she seems also to be the source of the summer lightning, not
its reflection, while

the same flashbulb catches a glimpse of the blood
behind my eye. I'm
demon-eyed, but I'm
also filled with acceptance.
Look.

My expression.

In it you can see a frozen horse, and
a frozen field, my
country's wars, and
my own child's future in my
own tyrant's eyes.

1

(are gone)

Perhaps

this is what it feels like to be a woman
who is also a vulture. To be a vulture

who is a woman

with a broken wing.

To have been
cared for
by a mother. To have
hatched. To have
been

featherless as a girl.
To have been fed
the death of others
by a mother
in a nest.
And then

to have grown feathers.
To have been
sent out
on her own.

Not to have wanted to go.

But to have flown.

To have already known

the scent so well
she can smell it
as herself.

The eavesdropper (or what I thought I heard my mother talking about on the phone, in another room, thirty-six years ago)

I still keep it hidden in the jar of saltwater you gave me   don't worry   no one can hear me   my husband's in the bathroom and my daughter's in her bedroom   wearing those headphones made of sponges on her ears

Yes, I've kept it all these years, and kept it hidden   but—I have to tell you something:

Something about it   recently   has changed   since we last spoke

The shell has opened, and—

How?

Calm down   please   I'll tell you   I've waited years to tell you   I couldn't call—I don't know where you live   I don't even know your name! So   I'll tell you now:

The gluey seam that held it closed?   Well   at some point   that seam began   to dissolve

I don't know   how or when   it might have begun around Christmas-time some year when I was still so busy with   gifts   and children   too busy to notice

But it was gradual   also   and subtle   not something anyone could easily have seen happening   through the water   through the glass   inside the jar we wanted to keep it in   forever   so I don't know   perhaps it was earlier than that   I only know that when I first noticed—I—(*of course* it's still alive   how do I know?   *because I know*)

So   after the seal first began to loosen   everything accelerated   and after that   I could see inside it   and what I saw was   (yes   of course) a tongue of it   but pale—this tongue   it was white as a strip of paper also smooth   no bumps or grooves   but there was no doubt about it: this was a tongue

8

I'm sorry to use the past tense   I use it so you might better understand
how it appeared to me when it was all still so   new   so strange   to me
to describe it to you as well as I can   what I saw then   its   simplicity
and then   its gradual shift into familiarity

Now I spend an hour with it every morning   and if the weather's mild
at night   after they've gone to bed I take it out and lie on my back   in
the grass   and balance the jar on my chest   and then   together   we
watch the metallic flower petals spin into one another through   that
dangerous memory   of heaven   which is   I suppose   the past

Please don't cry   it's not your fault   no one is to blame   and nothing
has truly been ruined   nothing at all   nothing's wrong   there's no dis-
comfort   I'm sure of this—no pain   there's only time left now   which
is letting something loose   looser   inside it   inside us all

No   don't worry about that   I've made the preparations   I promise
yes   when I die it will die also

And she can't hear me   I'm sure of it   she isn't listening   and even if
she is   well   then   the eavesdropper's punishment is hers   she can't be
spared it   all her life will be spent with her breath held   trying to hear
it   only to hear   in the end   the sound of moss stuffed into the ears
of a stillborn kitten

Think of it!

For the rest of her life   whether she's at the kitchen table or in line at the
store with her groceries   always to be listening to those tapes of a con-
versation she recorded with the microphone she slipped into her mother's
coffin   into this grave   thirty-six years ago

Well   she'll find no meaning in that silence   although she'll search for-
ever for the jar in which she'll remain so certain   it must still float: the
tongue of her mother's ghost

The time machine

My mother begged me:
*Please, please, study
stenography.*

Without it
I would have no future, and this
is the future that was lost in time to me
having scoffed at her, refusing
to learn the only skill I'd ever need, the one
I will associate forever now with loss, with her
bald head, her wig, a world
already gone
by the time we had this argument, while
our walls stayed slathered in its pale green.

While we
wore its sweater sets. While we
giddily picked the pineapple
off our hams with toothpicks. Now
I'm lost somewhere between
1937
and 1973. My
time machine blown off course, just
as my mother knew it would be.
Oh, Mama: forget about me.
You don't have to forgive
me, but know this, please:
I am
the Stenographer now.
I am

the Secretary you wanted me to be.

I am
the girl who gained the expertise you

knew someday some man would need.
Too late, maybe.
(Evening.)
I'm sick, I think.

You're dead.
I'm weak.

And now
I'm going to tell you
a little secret.

Get out your pen and steno pad.
Sit down across from me.
Are you ready?

The grieving:
It never ends.

You learn a million
tricks, memorize
the symbols &
practice the techniques
and still you wake up every morning
lost inside your
lost machine. Confused, but always
on a journey.
Disordered.
Cut short.
Still moving.
Keep speaking
Mama.
Please.
I'm taking it down
so quickly, so
quickly, even (perhaps especially)
when I appear

not to be.
I do this naturally.

See? In the end, no
training was needed.

None at all.

None at all.

I taught myself so well.
It's all I can do now.

Two canoes

Look: I'll show you again. There she is. Tied to a dock, aging at the end of a rope. Or lost in open water. What's the difference? The stars glint overhead like fish. The fish, like stars, swim under and around her—silver & finned & wriggling in their skins. Yes. Look: these writhing stars have been slipped into the whole idea of *fish,* except that fish . . . well, their flesh was zipped up far too hastily, too clumsily, for this. If you try to hold one to your face & kiss it, like a slap, you'll understand. Since—

Since it's not a fish. It is the muscle plucked from the arm of a strong man as he paddles, or as he takes a swig from a flask, or when he swings a bat—& you thought you could hold a thing like that? Well, the next time you forget what it's like to lie down with such an impulse, close your eyes. I'll show you again.

The interview

A: Well, I suppose I had some premonitions. Sure. Maybe. Doesn't everyone?

Q: When?

A: The day before, I guess? Two days? (Shrugs.) Not sure.

Q: And these premonitions consisted of—?

A: I think I looked outside the kitchen window that morning and saw a stranger in the daisies. Gray suit. Standing there, staring.

Q: Staring at—?

A: Me. He was staring at me staring at him.

Q: Through the kitchen window?

A: Yes.

We thanked the victim for his time.
We let him go back to the parking lot, to his wife.
We wished him
good luck before we remembered, and then we congratulated him
on his good luck
instead.
He asked
if we'd like to speak with him again, and we
said no, we didn't wish to speak with him
again.
He seemed
disappointed then, but we were disappointed too.
He'd been
correct, of course. Who
has never had a few such premonitions?
A stranger or two in the daisies, or wearing

high black boots in the rose
garden or behind a tree. We've

all lived all this time
in this same suburb. But

somehow
we'd expected more
from him
than from ourselves.

Unlike us, this man had been
struck
by lightning
without
even knowing it

until he noticed
that his shoes had been
unlaced, removed, set
down on the sidewalk beside his face

carefully (it seemed) while
smoke rose out of them, and
out of him, and then

he knew
he was still alive, although
he couldn't hear
his heartbeat
in his chest, he said.
He'd been

kissed
and also killed
in a single incident. God
entered and exited him, and
he hadn't felt it. All

he could remember was
some strangers, the other day, standing
in some daisies. Black boots. A band
played an anthem. It seemed to him to be
marching in his direction.

Well, we figured
the stranger was just a neighbor, and
the boots came out of his imagination.
The anthem
was being played
by the high school marching band
on the football field at halftime.
And the daisies—they
were planted by his wife
one spring, and ever since then
they'd come back. Just
some ordinary variety. The usual
white petals circling one
blind yellow eye.

We caressed the pens
in our pockets
as we stood at the window
after he left.

We watched him
cross the parking lot
to the car where
the wife
waited for him.

Or, we assumed
the woman waiting for
him was his wife.

In truth, for all we
knew, she could have been
anyone, waiting
anywhere, for
him, or for someone else.

Eleven girls

Eleven girls go
to the forest
to pick wildflowers. They

laugh at an old woman
on the path. Imagine

tall trees—thin trunks, ragged bark, pine needles—
as eleven girls keep walking, how the forest grows darker.
Beds

of needles. Shady moss. And darker. And darker. But

all of this takes place
in an innocent era, with girls in forests never
expecting to be raped
or murdered. This

takes place in some old country, maybe the one
our great-grandparents
came from, with customs, prohibitions, metrical
charms, violent folk songs and nursery rhymes.
So when

the old woman turned around and shouted to them, "Hand
over your souls to me!" of

course the girls
laughed, but when
they'd ended their laughter and her hand
was still held out, they saw
she meant it: she was a witch

or something like a witch.
But she was only one.

And they
were eleven.

They ran
at her, tore
her to shreds
with their

bare hands, scratched out her eyes
with their fingernails, beat her
with branches they broke
from the trees, so when

they left the forest, their baskets
held not wildflowers, but scraps
of that old woman instead. Gray

hair, down to the roots, in handfuls. Two

eyeballs, and an earlobe, and a tongue, and
one of the eleven girls kept
for the rest of her life
a nipple to give as a wedding gift to her son
(her only one)
and to his bride
on their wedding night.

She told them she'd bitten it off
with her own teeth
when she was a girl, not much younger
than they were.

How sharp her teeth had been back then!

"Give me your souls," she said to them.
They laughed. Surely
this was a joke. This

was long ago.
The Past.
It was

shriveled from the beginning, but what
would you expect it to look like
after so many years had been
given up in exchange
for your soul?

Like wildflowers, or like
an old woman's nipple?

When a bolt of lightning falls in love

with an old woman, sex is reinvented
as the world's first toaster oven.

When lightning falls in love with a middle-
aged woman, lightning gives

birth to an electric guitar. When
lightning falls in love

with a married man, his wife becomes
an arsonist. When lightning falls

in love with an arsonist, she
gives birth to a son. When

lightning falls in love with my son, I wake up
to the streaking-comet scream of the fire alarm

in the hallway of a motel
on the wrong side of an ocean, and

I think, Thank God. I think: All
this lightning has always had

a plan, and if lightning can make plans, as if
lightning goes on, like lightning's plans, and

will go on
long after I've gone—then

my own lightning's work here
is almost done.

Storm

A gray car driven by a woman in a gray hospital gown, through
the good part of town, where the bad things happened.
Then, not now.
Now, she can drive anywhere
she wants. Over
bridges, through forests, across golf courses. She can spew
all the velvet green of that damp grass onto the golfers and watch
as they duck and run, hear
them swear at her, while the earth slops down on them from the sky.

She has a steering wheel, a gas pedal, a full
tank, so
despite the prognosis, she
can splash through the sacred puddles all she likes. She can
roll down the windows and smell the Band-Aids that have
steeped in those puddles along with overripe pears and oily rope
for a week, since the storm, before
the freeze. She
drives 100 mph down the freeway
in the beginning of the first blizzard of the season, and feels all the sea-
creature pores that live on the
surface of her skin open their mouths to cry out a film of something
very sweet. It coats
every bit of her. And she remembers then: that
rich lady with her rose water chilled in a freezer. That rich
lady whose laundry she used to fold after school for a dollar. How

much of that rose water that rich old lady had, but
she still noticed when a bottle of it was gone.

Eventually (yes, this thief is me, of course) I can't see
a thing ahead of me. The windshield wipers just
confuse me. The dark they reveal
beyond the glass is worse than any starry speculation

could ever be. I don't mind dying, but I'd prefer to avoid the fame
that attaches itself to the name of someone who kills
someone else
with her car. So I slow down.

Once (this
memory could be
another false one) I caught, with one
hand, a hummingbird in flight, like
a poor prognosis, I suppose, or a large
inheritance, perhaps, and I chose

to keep this information
to myself.

I wrapped her in
my mother's favorite scarf—which was
green, dime-store
satin. Too

tightly, I regret.
(I was a child.)

But before she died, I named her
Little Storm and kept her under my pillow where I could listen
as she repeated
her name
as loudly as she could (in silence) every
night for the rest of my life.

My silk scar

The one I wear
around my neck—

No, I meant
my silk *scarf*—although

I wore no scarf. Not then.

It was summer
behind the indoor
high school swimming pool
on the other side of the parking lot.

He knocked me off my bike. (I don't remember this, but it was in
the paperwork, which I kept for decades in a folder in a closet until
I asked my husband to burn it
for me, and I know he did because I watched him from the kitchen
window and saw the ashes on the sleeves of his jacket when he came
        back in.)

The frame was bent.
My bike.
A Schwinn.
Emerald green.
I think I had a towel
in a basket between
its handlebars.

He knocked me off.
The frame was bent.
(I don't remember this.)
A neighbor fixed it for me, but if
I ever saw that bike again, I also don't remember that. But I do
remember my father, how
we'd hear him in the bathroom, how he sounded as if he wept

for all the world-without-him-in-it, which
one day the world would be: he
loved me so, so much.

And my mother woke me up
to tell me it was time for swimming lessons again.
Yes, I got raped, but, still, I had to learn
to swim.

I could show you where it happened, but what I wish—
What I wish is I could let you see the light that day
the way I did:
that light lasted only half an hour or so, I suppose, but
afterward it lasted my whole life. Whenever
I want to see it I just close my eyes, and then
it pours all over me

in tubs and buckets and trunks of light emptied all at once
all over what was just (in my case) some
eleven-year-old girl who'd stumbled
into a convenience store
where a boy I never saw before
or again
left the register, locked
the door, told me to sit down on the floor while he called—

I don't remember this, but I remember (will not forget) that
he asked me what my favorite flavor was before he got me some-
thing cold to drink, for free—with a straw, because
it was broken, my jaw, which
I remember now and then
when I bite into an apple or open
my mouth too wide
to yawn. Now, just

that flavor is a secret I'll
never tell anyone again.

What it was.
What it still is. It's

sacred, that secret and what I tasted
then, behind the locked door
of the convenience store, on
the other side of the high school's indoor
swimming pool
across from the
parking lot
where he told me
to shut up, and still (I don't know why)
I didn't.

I asked
if I was dead
or going to die. "No," the boy said. "It's
not that deep, the cut, but you'll need some stitches."

And he was right, unlike
my rapist, who told me he was
killing me, and then
that I was dying
while he cut me
with his little knife—*superficially*—a word

I doubt I knew the definition of back then, but which
I've grown to know
the meaning of
a little better every year I go on living. This

death of mine, it took
a doctor only seven stitches
to sew it

back into me again. And
with such precision! Now
I have only

this silk scar.
My rapist

never touched my scarf
because I wore no scarf.
My rapist
raped me, and he
didn't
get away with it.

Secrets

A bear eating various bald vegetables in a cage off the freeway
next to a gas station. You
saw this as a child. Patches of raw flesh. A desperate loneliness.

You can live with such a thing most days, as well as your
neighbor does, the one
who ran over
his daughter's cat. He
confessed it to you, weeping, begging
you to keep his secret, since
he told his wife and children that the cat
had run away, apparently
unhappy, looking for a better place.

You watched his little girl staple
posters—LOST CAT—to every
telephone pole in the neighborhood, and promised
you'd call her if you saw her cat.
Can you live with that?

Of course you can.

But one dark night
a new
comet appeared in the sky—some

streaming, speeding ball of dust and ice. Your husband
put on his jacket, went outside. You

didn't, never
wanting to have to think
about a thing like that
in some future you preferred
not to imagine. So

you stayed inside, and when
he came back to bed, so excited, you

wouldn't even let him describe it.

The house sitter

I wake from a nap in another family's house, with
their dog snoring beside me, their
tiny clocks everywhere, chiming. This

is not my house, I have to remind
myself. This is only my confusion. And this

green lace passing over this cheese in this refrigerator
does not belong to me. This

sound of this ceiling fan is theirs, not mine.

But they've left me so much bliss to contemplate:
It should be obvious to me, of course, that
in another year they'll be divorced. All of this, they'll
split it up, I guess.
But not with me.
Between themselves.

Still, I own it all
this afternoon. All
of it. The whole

place (I'm not
making this up) smells of roses. And this
chaos of birds in the backyard at all these feeders.
All these seeds, just
set out for these strangers, for free.
Wings and songs are all they receive for all of this, as
if nature itself sent these friends of mine some special
message, which
they themselves might need to hear, as they, it seems
have chosen, themselves, not to breed. Or

not with each other at least. Or

not yet, which will
become, sooner or later, never. Not

that it's any of my business, my
friends' fertility.
And both of them left-

handed, too, apparently.

A coincidence?

And readers. On every
flat surface there's some book I should
probably bother myself to skim
at least. No

wonder they'll fall so
quickly out of love! So

many possibilities! Who
has time in this life to do
all of this? All

of this requires
a second life, clearly.
Although for all I know, they're

completely content with this one.
More or less.
As it is. I've

peeked into their medicine chest
(of course: wouldn't anyone?), and it's

just so much hydrogen
peroxide, some cotton balls, a hundred
Q-tips. What

must all of those be for?

And where do they hide their Tylenol, their
dental floss, their Prozac, their Adderall?

Perhaps these things travel along
with them when they leave, or maybe
they decided (not unwisely) to put their prescriptions
somewhere I couldn't see
them. The temptation, which I'm not denying
there would have been.

But no, there are no hiding places here, it seems to me.

My God, their freezer!
Nothing in it! This
freezer is a Hollywood horror movie scene . . .
The Fog. The Scream.

Although, in their refrigerator—as
I cannot manage to
force myself to forget, nor
make peace with, nor
throw it away, for
myself if not for them—there sleeps
this wedge of cheese, which, naturally, after

so many years has become a bit
like a child by now. Or

at least it seems like a child to me—
something
biological, ever changing, quickly
outgrowing its little crocheted gown of green.

Someday someone will need to name
it, feed it, pick it up from school
eventually. Their

little blessing, or
terrible miscalculation.

And someone's already watered down the vodka
in the pantry, that's for sure. However—

such tidiness, such hygiene. With

the sole exception of what I fear may be a pubic
hair—hers or his—clinging to a pink

bar of soap in a shell-shaped dish, this

bathroom could be a Scrubbing
Bubbles advertiser's dream.

Also, their silverware is
silver, literally—
Yes, silverware

in both fact and theory. And
polished. And
gleaming. Nothing

here needs to be more clean. So

(could she have believed I wouldn't read it?)

I spend all morning and a cup of tea (these
brittle cups, like holding air
that's holding tea!) with her diary:

Nothing in it, really.
Not a clue. No

future, no present, not even
any memories. Just, every single day, a few

more simple facts. The weather, changing. Her
weight, unfluctuating. Some story from the newspaper.
Boy on a rampage. Prisoners escape again. Or

how her mother called, what her mother said.
Mostly, "Nothing's
new with me. How about
with you?" Only

one recounting of one
peculiar dream
in which a man she never names (and never
mentions again) makes

a surprise appearance in a parking ramp, and she
decides, in this dream, to trade
her car for his. And who

wants to hear, let alone read, about other people's dreams?
I slide it back behind the nightstand, where she
must have thought that she could
hide it from me.
How? Why? Then

I say aloud, to myself as well as to their dog: "I

must never leave this place." And then

to myself (silently, seriously) *I must
never come back to this place again
if I ever leave.* And

only then does it occur to me
to open the jewelry box
in the top drawer
of the dresser they seem to share
so equally—between her under-
things and his

socks. When
I lift the lid, see—

Oh, this is where they keep all
their damp and gleaming secrets:

The liver of a sparrow
The heart of a dove
The womb of a robin
A magpie's tongue

2

(have burned)

She asked me, "Did you cry then?"

when I cut that onion—all
its vulnerability, and nakedness, and the silence
with which it allowed itself to be
sliced into slivery ribbons, so
easily separated from and collapsing
away from
the center to which they had been
mindlessly and comfortably attached
since the beginning, and then

its pale, watery juice, how it
pooled around the halved bulb, which had
begun to swell in
winter, in the darkness, underground, in a garden—
expanding gradually, in rings and ringlets, and how
these grew larger and wider as they labored to hide
the sentiment
at the center of it, until

they were a singularity, finally, until
the whole of it was veiled, and vague, made
ambiguous by a parchment gown, that
bit of modesty
the world had left to it, like
the papery thing a gynecologist
might drape over your spread legs
before peering into
the secrets hidden between them. It's

not for nothing, that little
comfort offered—which
you must accept when
you are offered it—meant

to help you feel as if
you're cared for, so you
might imagine yourself then
shielded as you wait to be yanked

out of the earth by your hair
and then
your singularity, cut
in half, and then in half again, and then in half
again, and then—the tears, the
paper gown fallen
off of me
to the operating room's
luminous floor, and the knife
pressed into myself when she asked me, "Did
you cry then?"

"No," I said.

"Not even a little?"—until
nothing was left, until
the nothingness was what
was left, and we were just happy to have it, and
we both knew
what it was for, and the reason for the rest of it, what
that had always been—

the high heels, and the mascara, and
the panty hose, and the poems—

"I don't
think so," I told her.
Silence.
But she kept staring
into the hole, until, finally, I couldn't
fail to see
the open door through which she wanted

to lead me, so I followed her, obediently,
and said, "Yes. I cried
a little. But
I didn't feel sad."

True Crime (1)

A few days after her daughter's funeral, a bouquet of white roses was delivered in a long box to her front door. A small card was stuffed among thorns and petals, which card expressed something about pain giving way eventually to peace, and so on, in clumsy poetry.

Wrapped in tissue, without a vase. It was as if some kind of romantic gesture were being made, not just one more floral arrangement meant to be set beside the coffin of the murdered girl, but to be delivered

to her resurrection.

How sugary they looked, how spun—created out of ideas a girl might clip from magazines (*Elle, Cosmopolitan, Seventeen*) not grown in a garden or even a greenhouse but in some factory where lacy bras and panties were stamped and stitched by other girls, far away, who could never leave but were not called slaves, whispering to one another across the conveyor belt before being shipped off in hot-pink plastic to some imaginary shopping mall in a country made of imagination.

She thought how her daughter would have liked these roses best of all, before she saw—

A beetle, neon green, the size of a pencil eraser or a beauty mark, clawing itself out of the center of some daydream, like a girl being chased through a forest, pursued by

an inspiration,
a man with a knife,
and a bouquet.

Blindside

There would have been jets
at my conception. Jet engines and bombs on jets. Jets full of

uniforms and men, and then my father & my mother, in some
bedroom of some apartment

owned by the government, with
the window wide open and the sound of the sound of children

pretending to kill one another.
That was Louisiana, some air force base. It's here on my

birth certificate. See it? But, botanically, I was born
into the Club family of mosses. A spore gone off

on her own, stupidly, thinking
about luck. Good luck! It was low, damp, chilled, where

I was formed out of lust and the kind of insult to one's
most beloved, that sort

of closest to the bottom—I'm never going to go. My
ancestors got on a boat and crossed the ocean

to get away from it, and also
from the hunger that was the hunger of the first of the

several hundreds of other hungers. And then
it was very quiet (at home) for sixty years.

"Do you recognize this man?" my mother asked me as she
held a photograph up for me to see.

It was a cheap copy of an evil book, silvery and lying open
on the floor beside my lover's bed.

The light bounced off it all. Off all
of it. Forced me to read the words I never wanted to read

before or again: *the storm puts its mouth to the house and* . . .
He was that boy. He was back.

I wanted to cut his ponytail off and carry it with me, in
my purse, my pocket, stuffed

into my bra's cups, take it out, press it to my
lips, this strangeness that came out of him, which

passed through his skull into the world, growing
so long he had to tie it with a rubber band

behind him, where all day
it caressed his neck. I told my mother, "No."

She said, "Look closer. Hold
the photo to your face. Close

your eyes. Now take the deepest
breath you've ever taken in your life, and then—"

Red Mud Lake (1)

Two sloppy fistfuls of friendship left
after all the lies. To wash
the red mud of it
off in a lake
of red mud. And then

to shake your wet hands around you in the air
to dry them. The droplets fly, lit up by
so much sun. They
spark. A bunch of little just-
struck match tips in search of
a firestorm to
start. As if we'd soaked a bride's
veil in kerosene, after which one of us held the eye
of a cigarette to a lacy thread, so
the whole thing
went up in flames

in a flash
almost too fast
to see it coming, followed by
the slow-motion drift
of its greasy innocence
on a breeze, until the ashes
settled on the waves
of Red Mud Lake.

Even if we
wanted them back, along with our secrets, we
could never fish them out
of that bad water—the deepest, the darkest, the
muddiest lake of them all, the lake
the muskrats go
to die in, the lake in which the bones of corpses

dissolve into cattails to become
lily pads, tadpoles, one lost glove.

But don't think
about this—
or about—
or—
love. You'll
lose your nerve.
Close your eyes instead, just long enough
to count to ten. Then

say the name of your friend, one
last time. After that, recite

some clumsy rhyme for her, while you wade
into Red Mud Lake, and then

go back to shore. Forget
all about what you said to her before

you wade into its even
redder mud again.

An evil meal

Like an evil meal being served to someone who hasn't eaten in weeks . . .

Like veal, I suppose—the youngest and most tender of all meats, being,
        as it is, the flesh of a creature that only
once or twice managed to struggle onto its vague legs, smell the breeze,
        briefly wondering.

This world, an imagination locked into a calf-sized cage.

And the weasel with blood on its small, sweet face, darting across the
        field with the chicken still held in its teeth.

But what is a weasel to do after stumbling upon an untended flock of
        deliciously flightless things? How lovely the little bits and pieces.
        How sweet the eye socket. Also the marrow in the bones of that
        hen's feet.

Such intricacy. Whole cathedrals devoted to ever more fleeting beliefs.
        In ancient cities there were winding streets that lead to beliefs
        like these.

Advertisements for things we longed to buy, or drive, or kill and eat—
        these desires were set into us, deeply, by people more beautiful
        than we could be.

Until there was, finally, no difference between what we thought we
        wanted and what we needed.

What we believed became the truth, until they told us no longer to
        believe it.

To speak

with gratitude to Scott Lyons

Like a cradle carved out of air, as
it was becoming, although it was always there.

This language, given to us to share.
Once, it swayed
above the world—Sumerian, free, belonging to all
creatures equally, being

all we'd ever needed: one
another's names, our own, the names we called
our places:

Home, Prison, Hospital, There.

And our mountain passes, as well. *Do Not Go There.*
And other warnings:
Stop. Wait.
Take. Eat.
*Don't die on us, Buddy. Hang on. Hang on. Breathe. You
aren't going to leave us. Don't
you dare—*

Our rivers, too: Nile, Danube, Yangtze.
When one of us pointed in the direction of Leech
Lake, we each knew what it meant (*lake full of leeches*)
before anyone had to tell us. And

we knew why, once, and also where. The language
we shared!
It was a baby in a cradle. After
centuries, it became words
pulled out of a cradle
and became a civilization—

which we forgot to thank a god for. A god we forgot
to praise. So, what did we expect but to be

abandoned by it in the end? And now, here

we are, left with only the few things left between us
we can agree on:

*Coca-Cola, Don't Touch the Roses, Open Your Mouth
and Take Your Pills. Suddenly.*

You mean—?

Yes, I mean it. I mean

look how far we've come in peace. See
how long we searched for you
out there in the thick
sweet space between us. It took

centuries to find you. The invention
of radio telescopes. We invested so much time
and money to listen
to that heaven, and
most of us died in the silence you sent back, until—

one of us leaned forward. One of us finally stopped
and said, "Listen—"

We did.

"Do you hear it?"

We didn't.

"What does it sound like? What is it?"

You said, "It's the sound of a hoofprint
left in the muck

outside the broken gate of some
homely beast's
empty pen."

Yes. We
could hear it then
as it spoke to us as if
we were its children, or the gravestones of its children—

Or the stones we'd so lovingly placed above the graves
of our own children's pets. (*Here lies
Enfant, the good
dog we'll always love.*)

How little we could say to them. Those
expressions. That
incomprehension. How

they died on tables, needles injecting into them
all that was left to be said. Or under
the tires of a truck after

they stepped out of their pens.

All that love we tried to communicate to them.
The comfort they heard, perhaps, in the sloppy
syllables spilling out of our mouths.

"What is it saying to us?"
This, we asked of the only one of us who understood.

"It says, 'I'm telling you now, forever:
I never—*never*—wish to speak to you again.'"

Neighbor (1)

You told me where you hid the spare
key, under
the welcome mat. The lacy

curtains in her bedroom windows: you let them blow
in and out
with the
breeze. I was watching. Waiting
for a sign, and then

one day a single strand
of her hair entered
my front door, stuck
to the damp pink asshole
of my one hound.
I still have it.

There were still
the feathers, so I can see now how you could
so easily pretend
that the rest of her was still
there when you got back
from your bottles with your friends
on the patios of the houses in the foothills, or
still coated with the clamminess of your love affairs
and layovers (so many
grounded jets in so many
airports between
your tours and conferences).

You grew fatter, fatter, older. Your
children wept
when you called them
to say goodnight from
somewhere. Then

they were drunk and drugged. Dressed
up in their expensive
suits and dresses
in their caskets
after their overdoses.

But I was an artist too.
I left my paintings for you
to hang in your living room.
On the back I wrote, *A gift
for you, my
lovely neighbors
and for your
lovely daughter.*

I called one of them
Snow on the Mountain.
Another, *The Nude:*
a girl in a bathtub reclines, legs
spread as she
washes herself between them with a fish.

Or *Summer Lightning.*
The same girl. Now, she reads a little book
as she sits alone in a park
wearing a dress the same powder blue as the sky
behind her in the distance, where
the aspens shiver their anxious little hands, all
gloss and green, all over her, and that man—

That man behind her—

That's the electricity
you never noticed
was your neighbor, the one

who would animate your daughter into life
from the dead bits you left behind.

Yes.
I lived beside you all her life.
When she wore that dress.
The wedding.
That champagne and watercress
and, to be even more
exotic, instead of rice
you bought butterflies
to toss into the air
after the vows were taken.

But some had been delivered already
dead, or dying, tucked inside their
waxy envelopes
by the party planner. Joke
on you.
A damp wing's final spasm
in a wedding guest's hand—a scrap
of uneasy laughter.

After the feast
I gave you back what was left
of her for the funeral repast.

Yeah.
I was that neighbor.
The one to whom you called out
Hey! How's it going?
when you took out the trash.
Or, in the morning, holding your
coffee mug in one hand
while still in your pajamas, and
a paperback tucked under your arm.

Great! I always said.

I always was.

And I still am.
Right next door:
A fact you chose
so long to ignore, there's no
reason to stop pretending.

We were practically friends!
We're still
almost friends now. You

borrowed my hammer
when you lost yours.

I raped your daughter.

No elegy

No. No elegy. Instead, the car
stalled on the freeway, the passengers
departed and the driver fled.

The driver, who was my friend, who
wanted once, and was, who

dreamed and drove and listened
to stupid music on the radio.

Who waited, who ate, who
spoke and spent and finally arrived
at the foreign country
that bore his name—
and of all the choices
he ever made
there were three choices left:

Violence, illness, old age.

No. No choice:
You refused, of course, to make it. Sailboat
slipping under a wave, you
swam away, or

you were rescued by a boat captained
by sorrowful ladies
of a certain age
who would love you as you'd never
been loved enough in life—

as mothers, or lovers, or the slow
passing of certain summer days.
Their parasols, your shade.

And my little candle stub
in a great cathedral, and
the prayers I sometimes remember
to say, and

the long, low, beautiful notes of a bassoon being
played by a terrible thing—

No. Not even this
I know!
A bird!

A bird that makes its nest
in the highest towers
of the children's hospital
out of the softest
children's hair.

You

loved nothing better than a lovely terror—

Yes. That nest. That nest
is where you are.

The Nostalgia for Infinity

name of an ancient spaceship used to escape the planet Resurgam to travel to Yellowstone in search of a new captain after their own contracts the Melding Plague, in the novel Revelation Space *by Alastair Reynolds.*

Before he launched it, our father said to us, "Calm down. This isn't
going to be like Vietnam or something. You kids have no idea
how lucky you are." We did

have Kool-Aid, and little waxy Dixie cups
to drink it out of and then to throw out
of our spaceship's windows into

the vacuum, where there wasn't a single sound wave, so no one
could have heard our screams or songs or whether
we played the radio too loud and sang along. Except for him. I had

a friend back then, on Earth, who'd had for a pet a skunk
that had been de-scented. It was always
vanishing. It hid

between couch cushions, in kitchen cupboards, in
boxes of Saltines, until
finally it hid in the freezer in the basement. No one knew

how it got in there, or what to do. What *does*
one do with a frozen loved one after it's become
a curled-up handful of solid blood, stiff fur, tail permanently

lifted in a threat to all its enemies, snarling, snarling, smiling.

Well, one does nothing.
One follows one's father's instructions and marches onto the ship
without asking questions, and buckles up.

He told us, "If
you play that song one more time I'm gonna pull this thing over and kick
you out of it," so we turned it off. But it was

still there, being sung, but not with sound. This
was a very sad song about a boy who died
too young. He sang of all the pleasure he had taken

in being alive, on Earth: *We had joy, we had fun. We
had seasons in the sun.*

"For fuck's sake," our father said and squeezed
the steering wheel until we could see
how white, beneath the flesh, his knuckles were.

But we'd already turned it off. "In my day," he

told us, "there was a thing called napalm."
And then: "You kids ever hear
about a little thing called *napalm*?"

We were afraid to answer him.
We feared silence.
He explained:

"It attaches itself like a second skin, a whole
new skin
made of plastic wrap, microwaved, so you
can never pull it off yourself without also
pulling off yourself."

We learned to live in silence then. Until
our mother asked him could she smoke a cigarette.
We didn't hear his answer, but he must have said "No," since
we saw her put to her lips her fingertips instead
of a cigarette, and then she put the tips

of her red-painted nails
between her teeth, after which, we heard
nothing for several light-years except the sharp
trigger-snap, again and again, as she sat

beside him in our spaceship gnawing
her claws down
to their sharpest bits, and then

down to the quick, and then
down to the nostalgic
meat under it, while
we traveled on.

My first mistress

My first mistress was a mirror.
Thin as winter, and an heiress.
When I smiled at her, she smiled, and

when I grimaced, she grimaced. When
I cried, she turned my tears to silvered
strangers in the distance.

My shining party dress inside her.
My staggering drunkenness.

And when I slipped a new pair of shoes on my feet
and fell down wearing them, she fell with me, and then
we rose up together and limped home to him. When

they took off my breasts, she became
the surface without expression that let
me stare, and never said, "What

do you think you're staring
at in here?" Instead, she
polished my face softly with a cloth, and then

I screamed that I was dying. And then
I turned my back on her
while she was crying, after which

she reminded me, quietly, again: *Please
don't forget to turn
the light off when you leave.*

(will burn)

For the return of the bee

after Bill Abernethy's translation
of the Old English charm

Repeat, repeat, repeat:

Lord Christ, where is our bee?
She who stole the sugar bowl, sucked
lingeringly from the pink rose every spring, licked
the sticky bottom of the brandy snifter clean?

You shall not escape me, nor ever be free of me.

The way our words linger now forever in the ether.
Just try to snatch back a single
one of your own little secrets.
Once, I tried, and my
fingers glittered for a minute against the computer screen.
Then, nothing, permanently.

Return, return, return to me.

Even a can of frosting from the pantry.
Even the Sweet 'N Low packets beneath the sink.

Surely she who was its source could not also be its thief.

So, where can she be hiding now that nothing
disappears, or goes unheard, unseen. For we

can listen to our enemies whispering on mountain peaks.
We can place a target on the heart of any
anarchist, imam, member of the Tea Party, and even
through the deep

privacy of the sea

we can send a wave of electricity
smooth as a memory:
And I myself have witnessed

a miracle as it was happening:

a child in the backseat
of a car in a parking lot
behind a bar
waiting for his father
in the middle of the night, while the whole
thing was being filmed by
a satellite in the sky—
by what that child must have believed
to be a star.

Red Mud Lake (2)

That little scrap of friendship that was left behind after all the lies.
To wash it in a puddle full of feathers and
blood and vinegar and popular muffled music on a transistor
radio for the last time. And then

shake it out. Let the droplets fly around in sunlight like matches in search
          of fire.
Let them ignite. Let them say whatever's been so long on your mind. They

know wreckage, waste, burning
upholstery—how it smells when the sofa cushions start to smolder
and writhe, how the mirage of one final exhalation rises as
a greasy rainbow, or quavering gas-fueled bridal
veil, or

false smile, shroud, or prayer made out of petroleum
and resentment, down to ashes. Not

toxic, exactly.
Just too much prismatic
rippling. You couldn't stand it. You could no longer recall
what the definition
of it was:

to abide, to despise, to love, to make noise, to tell your secrets to one person and
          to want
your secrets back, to have thrown handfuls of yourself into a lake, for

the lake to have been yourself.

Toss it anyway.
Aim for the center. This is the muddiest lake on a planet
full of lakes
and mud

and red mud, out of which
the weeds grow
and rot, collapse, ferment, the lake

where the coyotes go to die. Don't
think too hard about that.
You'll lose your nerve.

Don't lose that too.

The dog, it's
about to bite you.
The bright barbed wire coiled up in the garage
waits patiently for you to begin
your whole new life, or
to build a whole new prison.
Close your eyes, but

don't count to ten.
Instead, say the name of your friend, and then
recite some clumsy little rhyme for her again:

one for every year of your friendship. Each
rhyme is the last one, for the last time.

Neighbor (2)

There I was waving goodbye
to my own reflection
in the rearview mirror of that U-Haul you were driving, and even
to myself
I looked like a fool. When you were gone I went inside, slammed
the door behind me, got in bed, pulled
a pillow over my head until I could hear only the little feathers
inside of it
still trying, stupidly, to fly.

Or I stayed in the driveway
forever and watched
and listened.
I just
stood there and watched and listened to the sound a songbird might make
while its neck was being twisted.
        Unbearable. And musical. Helpless. But insistent. I drove that love
        for you as deeply as I could into my brain.
I watched
you pull into the street and drive away with the sort of screaming trouble
one will have
with a rented truck.
I should've gone inside, slammed the door, but I
was still waving goodbye.

I stood there and waved.
I stood there and listened.

"Could be the brakes," my father said. "Worn out pads. Or maybe
the fan belt, or the power steering fluid's low." He shook his head.
He said, "I don't envy him."

I knew nothing about motor vehicles yet.
I was fourteen.

I was in love with the married man next door, who
drove away with his family
to another state
(to escape me, I liked to tell myself).

Maybe I finally ran inside, got in bed, pulled that flock of ruined
goslings over my head.

Or maybe I just stood there
beside my father, and
didn't envy him either.

No, I stood there forever.
So now I'll never know
what happened next.

Moon Landing

Forgot my helmet. My suit. My oxygen tank. My boots. They
were exasperated. Couldn't find my keys. My purse. I guess

I left that in the car, must be on the passenger seat. My
iPhone. My bright experience. My blissful

wave through space. They said, "You have to stay
inside the capsule. We'll be back." I asked them why. They said,

"Gravity: there isn't any." But then I told them about an old
lady who sat next to me once on the subway long ago, when

I was only twenty-four or so, who told me, "Not a leaf, and not
a stream, just space reflecting meaning, which is

your memory, which you

begin to lose, but not
until you no longer need it."

A Girl's Guide to Color

Do you remember pleasure?
Your favorite sweater?
A flattering scarf, a smart
cap, a pair of stones

dangling from your earlobes?

What color was it?

There are certain colors we all want to touch
on the right girl at the right time. But great

care must be taken. Short
waisted, short legged? From

your hemline to your hat you must wear a single shade.

Plump?
Break it up. A bright
coat. Orange
belt. If

your complexion's ruddy: no green for you, and don't

forget—the darker the dress, the smaller and smaller
it will make you. Pastels, however, enlarge and age
you. Either

take advantage of pastels, or avoid them at all costs.

And, as gold is strictly for brunettes, dirty
blondes must not wear blue. Another

rule: lilac, coral, and chartreuse. And

O unlucky redhead, so many colors not for you.

Have you ever seen a sunset
clash with the sea or the sky?

Such is a redhead
in a yellow blouse
to the naked eye, and yet

so many girls make such mistakes
without ever knowing why, while

others seem as if they hardly
need to try. Witness

Cynthia, enchanting in her purple suit, high-
lights in her copper hair:

Cynthia would never wear rose and green together!
In fact, she's sewn this skirt herself, knowing
—as she knows instinctively so

many things—that there are lovely bits
and pieces of everything, and that
a girl can't simply buy these. She

needs to learn to make them for herself.

Take Cynthia as your model, then—and
as she has done, if
you need chiffon
get yards and yards of it at once, and then
divide it up among
all the girls in your club.

And when you one day stumble upon
those girls wearing
your chiffon, do not be jealous of them.

Do the stained
glass windows of Westminster Abbey
begrudge one another their radiance as
the sun passes from one to the next?

It's natural to be nothing, to become it. Just

do the best you can with what you have for
as long as you manage to have it, and

try always to remember how a color can
influence the mood of any man
who looks in its direction—and

knowing this, as you do now, decide
early in your life, would you rather

be a little jenny wren in winterberry red, or
a parrot
in a crate
stowed below
the ship's deck? Our

friend Kiki was born without a sense
of color, but
she has a sparkling laugh, and that's

all some girls will ever
need, wearing the dumpy
uniforms of their class, and

still a joy to see. But

let's be honest, shall we?
Which girl would you rather be—
Cynthia
or Kiki?

Would you paint the robes of the Virgin Mary
the red and black of a cancan dancer, or—?

This list grows longer as you grow older, but
you'll find it's
easy to memorize, and then
impossible to forget:

Too tall? Brown
jacket. *Big hips?* Never
a corsage of daffodils.
Are you a blocky girl?
If so, think
always of the cool
depths of Alpine
lakes. *Flat-
chested?* Avoid

the sky, the grass, the Pacific or Atlantic, as well
as any other great expanse, and you'll
be fine, most likely. Only

a few such simple principles, and
once you understand them, you'll
never need to crouch down and hold your

arms across your chest to hide your breasts again.
Or a hand between your legs to cover that. Have

you ever seen a maple tree in autumn try to disguise
the red of the leaves on its branches? Have you ever—?

Of course you haven't.

Now the men are almost done.

Admittedly, it's an odd
era in which to be a girl. So many options—

and not just fashion.
When they slam the door and toss you a towel, perhaps

you should feel grateful. (Do you?) When

one shouts, *Quit*
crying, slut—you

should probably do as he says:

Clean yourself up, Kiki.
Cynthia, you're lucky we didn't cut you.

Someday, you may feel blessed. For

now it might be best
just to get off the floor, get
dressed.

Some rules have been taken from the first chapter, "Color Magic," of *Teen-Age Glamor* by Mrs. Adah Broadbent (1955).

Talisman

Little tin key
lost somewhere in my memory, returned to me in a dream.

Like the blue-burning match blowing over the surface of
some drunk girl's sweet, flaming party drink. *Happy
birthday.* Lucky

coin rubbed away to nothing, turned back into invisibility.
Back into its first atomic energy. Both

lost forever now and all around me. I've
rendered it, it seems, back into its
first longing—to keep

safe the loved ones on the plane, or on the freeway, or
strapped to the gurney, opened for the surgery, wheeled
into the lobby, being

screened for the journey, or stamped with the date
at the entrance to the pool, the portal, the nightclub, or

any spot where one might pull to the curb, drop
off a soft target, kiss it, make
with it a plan to fetch it later—

unbloodied, still breathing, in no hurry. This
talisman with no magic. I've made it for you

out of your own flesh, teeth, hair.

Two gardens

I

In this one, the great man's statue lies facedown in the grass. Some
    butterflies.

In that one, a dish made out of bone sliced so thin that, held to the sun,
    it disappears—since
you can't hold a circle of light in your hand.

In the mud between these gardens, there are boot prints, but crossing
    the boundaries freely,
too, there are hundreds of long-necked birds (pink feathered) sipping
    honey
out of the hundreds of jars left out for them.

2

In one garden, this could be a generous impulse.
In that garden, there could be a trap.
Someone is a bird-watcher in this one.
Someone makes ladies' feathered hats in that. But

it's hard to tell the gardens apart from such a distance.
Still, there's definitely a fence between them, and the white slats of it
    appear to be painted with rosebuds from over here—although
    from over there, those

roses look like the small, red handprints of children
who came to this garden before us and bled.

Suffering song

This morning my past is a small chalk bird
in the hand
of Saint Francis, but my mind

is a closet full of gadgets:
smokeless ashtray, travel-
size defibrillator. All

these wild, black branches claw
at the purple sky.
See?
My backyard is also a machine.

So why didn't you
warn me, little eyeless bird
in the palm of a saint, if
you saw this coming?

Oh, she sings to me, *Eyeless
and mechanical:
Wind me up, you'll
see.* See?

In my poor translation, Montaigne
says that we pity
those who beg for mercy, but those
we spare
are the ones who threaten to rip us
to pieces with their teeth.

Therefore, if you listen you can hear
your own child's babbling creek
in the suffering
song of every creature you've eaten.

For a few minutes, once

I felt sure
that there were two of me. Extra arms. Extra
everything. For instance, sensations. I

heard echoes echoing me. And all my fears seemed to be

my freedoms too—being
duplicated somewhere, rapidly, in some
factory, as if by some
supernatural machine.

Or, perhaps, by some completely
ordinary machine, a change machine, a war
machine, a snow-in-the-deep-blue-of-evening machine.

I could
somehow drive my car while
also riding my bike. I
could walk a tightrope across two canyons while
sailing over myself, while walking
that tightrope. As

a jet's silver crucifix in the sky flies over me.
Or, snagged in electrical wires, a kite.
I was living my life a second time
for the first time
in my life, understanding
that I'd already lived a long time before I realized
that I was old enough by then to have been
my own daughter when my mother died.

Nine trials

1) A man on the sidewalk grabs his crotch just as a woman passes in a cab.

2) A girl is in the passenger seat of a car being driven by a friend who's talking on her iPhone. The girl knows she's going to die.

3) A very ordinary husband tells his wife about the ghost of a Civil War soldier he saw long ago. She knows it can't be true, but she also knows he isn't lying.

4) Woman on a train. Crude man beside her talks about her pussy before he starts to cry.

5) Girl with two boys in a crawl space. Stoned. They claim she brought them down here, so they want to know, now that they want to get out, why can't she find the door?

6) A newly married couple buys a pink house from an elderly woman. The husband says, years later, that he's never been able to sleep in the house, and his wife understands, suddenly, that by never he means *never*.

7) Woman meets her husband's best friend in a motel, clandestinely. He's exactly like her husband.

8) Woman married to a Vietnam veteran. His friend from the war visits, never leaves.

9) Man says he sees Jesus on the side of his toolshed, calls over all the neighbors, who also see it. The only one who can't see Jesus, although she tries and tries, is the man's second wife.

Rescue Annie

Resusci Anne . . . is a training mannequin used for teaching cardiopulmonary resuscitation (CPR) . . . [to] both emergency workers and members of the general public . . .[Her] face . . . was based on L'Inconnue de la Seine. *. . . the death mask of an unidentified young woman who may have drowned in . . . the late 1880s.* (Kpedia)

As silence, I carry inside myself
wet, white ashes. Smothered

school bells.
Swans at the bottom of a well.
Thunder under a mountain of rain-soaked party gowns.
The un-

performed caesarean section.

The small town
slumbering under
the avalanche. The sound

of the struggle ending

without a sound.

Unrequited love.

Fish full of water.

Bird full of feathers.
Mine, the most-
kissed lips on Earth.

Snapshots, last picnic

The whole bottle blown off
the picnic table by the wind.

The wine-soaked ground.

*

The sudden understanding
while I was trying to be happy:

Neither the pristine flesh
nor the flesh that's been
scarred, sewn closed.

*

We have been opened.
Rummaged through.
Spare parts incinerated.
Nothing will be left. Not

*

even toothless, artless, old, and
in debt. Not even
this fear of death.

Our friends, our forks, our

furniture, our pets.

*

Rain was followed, too late, by
sun, as the day went on.

Bomb angel

We made you.
We made you out of our
love for ourselves
and for each other. We collected, invented, or paid for
every single nut and bolt and nail stuffed into
the pressure cooker of you, after which
we slid it into a length of flesh, sewed

your eyelids closed. But the eyelids are transparent, as
you know. (See
how you see us waving hello?) You have hands made of
amphibian, philosophy, candor, plastic spoons, and
the kind of hard candy that tastes like
coffee, or rum—they are like the hands of salamanders, or
tongues. (Your

own tongue was the cat's
tongue once. Don't laugh.)
Your toes:
inexplicable, unexpected gifts from the enemy who was
my friend. Changeable, poor
sinners, doctor and lunatic, both of them. They
trade roles when they're bored: "Today

you crawl on the floor and tell me you're scared. I'll
watch you from this comfortable chair. Tomorrow I'll
come to the office with blood in my hair. You'll still be
the doctor. You'll ask me to calm down, although I'll tell you
that no one has ever felt calmer
than I feel now."

No genitals, of course. We wanted to spare you
the kind of human suffering we call
Privacy, or her cousin, whose name is sometimes
Mary Kate and sometimes Rope.

But your feathers!

They were never our idea.

All that feathery glamour attached itself to you
with no inspiration of our own, and without our permission.
One sunny day before you could remember anything, we
took you for a walk. You ran
ahead, faster than we could run, too fast to be caught
by us. When we found you, finally, you
were in the aviary
with the peacocks, and the nightingales, and
the strippers, and the drag queens, and the other angels in Las Vegas.

Feathers all over you, exploded
out of nowhere! Perhaps
we should've been concerned, but instead
we laughed and laughed.

We loved you.

We never
expected to own you. But
neither did we feel we owed you. We

were kind and loving creators.

Never owed you one thing.
Never asked to be repaid.
We felt
all of it had been a loan (except the feathers) to you.
But the wings they were made of are yours to keep.

Most butterflies become butterflies by wriggling
with no beauty or sense in the dark for a long time
only to live as butterflies for a week.
Some never even get that far. Some
are left naked, without hands or tongues or eyelids,

by their makers, and die as
squirming and confusion. That

could have been you.
But we wanted you to have
everything you might ever need. We wanted you
to have even more than you could possibly need.
We wanted to live long enough to see you become
at least
as lethal
as beautiful. We always knew you'd terrify
as thoroughly as you pleased. We knew
you'd wake up some morning and say, "I hate
both of you," and, although
we wouldn't believe it (*just
going through a phase; teens; they all go
through it; one day
your sweet little creature will become
your sweet little creature
again*), still

we'd also lie awake at night, too old and afraid to sleep—

and chained, and tied, and hand-
cuffed by age, by all we'd failed to do and
what we did, and seen
by you
to be unforgivable, make-believe, too
parental, too fond, too weightless—and, the worst of all, in
the way that anything wearing
its needs where others have to see them, obscene.

4

(have flown)

The beautiful hand

Never underestimate the devotion
of a god who gives birth in darkness
to his own likeness

by thought alone. You

were loved wildly before you even had time to open your eyes.

But now you can never catch up.
And that's the problem.
The gifts pile up, along

with the thank you notes you never wrote, or
wrote but never sent

to the parents
who adored you, to the friend
who cheated you, to the lover
on whom you cheated, to

the magician who thought he'd tricked you as he stood

on a stage in a puddle of his assistant's blood
for your entertainment only. Only
out of love. Like the ocean

to which you should have been
more grateful
as you waded into it.
It was every bit
as alive
as you were then, with its

purgatory of jellyfish, all
cloud and flesh and forgotten names—
passing between your legs.

Facts

for Jack

The housefly hums in the middle-octave key of F.
The average tongue of a blue whale weighs
more than an elephant.
Florence Nightingale kept
a small owl in her pocket.
A bear has forty-two teeth.
Schiller could write poetry only when he had
rotting apples in his desk.
It's against the law in Michigan
to catch a fish with your hands.
After he was stabbed, the last
words Caligula said were, "I am not dead."

And all the adjectives in the English language.
Also the flutter of the tiny fins
of the miniature blue fish in the aquarium
in the waiting room
of the dentist's office.
Saints, particularly
the celibate and female, always hide their eyes
from His radiance.
At least they hide their eyes the first time.
We don't know what they do after that.

The human soul has whiskers
longer than a cat's.
A cat's soul is a cloud full of claws.
The slowest
is always first—
young or old, sober or drunk, rich or poor. Always. When
you raise your arms to surrender to the police, your shadow
is briefly Jesus

behind you, but you can't see this.

Some words must never be separated, such as:
Blithe indifference
Blunt force trauma
Formless fruit
A shoe is tied by its laces to a branch of that tree.

A soggy Kleenex
has been stuffed beside the hymnal in the pocket of this pew.
Sewer grates.
Look down, you'll see
abandoned libraries beneath every city.

Google it.

There's something called *simple harmonic motion.*
I don't know what it means, but my guess is
it has to do with vibration, repetition, elasticity.
Hooke's law—
now, that's an actual thing. It means
that you can pull a spring too tightly, I think. And
you'll be sorry then.

$F = -kx$

Some numbers are all you needed.
I love you.
Hurry, but don't rush

to the exit
like everybody else, or you'll
be trampled too.
The Pandemonium.
The Stampede.
The glossy
green leaves of orange trees. Every single needle on this pine tree

has been shined today by the sun. The
rubber soles of athletic shoes. The steel toes of work boots. Forget
your possessions. Leave them. Nothing belongs to anyone now.
Just crouch
in a corner
or slip through the door that no one but you knows is hidden, but is
also wide open.

That's where I'll meet you.
That's where I'll wait. You'll
know how to find me because I'll be singing that song we heard
the drunk guy sing
on the bus that day, the last lines of which (please
let me remind you, whether you've forgotten
them or not) were these:

And a' the blood that's shed on Earth
Runs through the streams of that countrie.

True Crime (2)

She tucked her hair behind her ear, hoping he'd notice the earring—
little silver dove of it—and that maybe he'd also notice how her hair was
shining particularly that evening as she stood behind the cash register at
the hardware store, since she'd gotten up early to blow-dry it, since she'd
taken extra time with the curling iron, and then they hadn't had gym that
afternoon to fuck it up. Because

he was really, really looking at her.

And she was happy, at first, to be
sixteen, being seen.

The odyssey

So she rowed her little boat
back home
to Ithaca, alone, after

not having seen her own
image in a mirror for so
long she couldn't know
exactly how the sun and salt
had changed her face—no
more enameled cheekbones or
feathered eyelashes, almost

no eyelashes now
at all. And

her lips (once a bloodred bow)
now two scaly strips, chalk
white, thinned, meeting
in a stillborn's kiss.
And those

other lips, the labia—
withered, stinking, just
like every other flap and fold
of her, spoiled
cat food, woolly fish. And with
her fingers she could feel
the spillage of the pleats and scraps and
excess that was now her neck. No

mirror was required
to know
what a neck that felt like that
to her own touch
would look like

to a man. Nor
did she need to see her backside
now to know what it meant—
the pain that had grown
sharper and stranger
over the years
when she sat too long, even
in sand, in grass—that

she was no Callipygian now—
although she'd modeled
her buttocks for a sculpture of one
once, in a time that somehow
felt as if it hadn't
been so long ago.

But still she was so strong! Still, how
swiftly she could row! A man
her age would still—

Well, consider her husband, she supposed.
He'd be gray at the temples
and the testicles now. Eyes
a permanent, machinating squint. His
voice, wind sifted over inconsistent grit.
But some girls and poets
liked such men. That

sculptor's antlered hands
on her buttocks as he sculpted them.
Her stupid, candlelit sandals
on his stupid, little rug. She didn't

kid herself her husband had been
weaving and unweaving a shroud
or anything else
for twenty years while she'd been off

pursuing her career, even if she felt
she'd been doing it as much
for him as for herself.

Or that the dog
was still alive. Or that the swineherd
hadn't retired. Or that some new war
hadn't started, to which their son had not
happily sailed off, wearing a thin and shiny
breastplate, as easily pierced by an arrow as dive-
bombed by a gull.

But, like everyone else who's ever left
what she loved, she'd
woken up every fucking rosy-fingered dawn
and thought of them. And
now, finally, she was

close enough to see
the pale, familiar, ragged edge
of home, from which
she'd sailed away reluctantly, with so
much hope, and see, even
from this distance, how
it hadn't changed a bit.

Yes. *There it is.*
The oral tradition.
All its
bruising and creaming and blooming
and spuming onto the cliffs
and into the branches of the olive trees
and onto the flat, gleaming bellies
of the naked nymphs—all
our glamorous nonsense.
There it is again.

Of course, if she'd arrived, it would
have astonished all of them. After
all the places she'd been, after
the battles she'd fought, the honors
she'd won, she might have inspired
a hundred generations
of girls to follow her into that distance.

Instead, as
you know, she
slipped herself into the wine-
dark sea with her oars.

Of course, this choice was wrong.

So, let's say she didn't.
We weren't there, after all.
Okay.

Instead, let's say
a woman of a certain age
washes up on a shore
on a sunny day
instead of her empty boat
after twenty years away. She

steps up, looks
around, and—

well, here, I'm afraid, we
have to pause. In

this case, we have to pause
for centuries, I'm sorry, for
centuries filled with silence, without
immortalization

because a question occurs to her, just
as it occurs to us, and
no answer ever comes:

Where is the bard
who sings this song?

A doll's house

A little plastic bed, and at
the foot of it, a plastic cat.
The dresser with its seven drawers
that do not open up, of course.
The hollow stove, all square and pink.
The master bathroom's unplumbed sink.
In this, a debt the wife must pay.

A child she drove to school today.
A teapot. Sieve. A tiny broom.
A husband in a basement room.
This is the little dream they have.
This future they believe they have—
Willfully blind, they eat and fuck.
To wake and sleep, it is enough.
And always there's this untouched cake.
The TV's blank. The phone is fake.
The thing you never dared to fear
will never make its way in here.
So mostly you can just go on
moving your furniture around
while relishing your privacy
and privilege, while on her knees
some little girl considers these
bitter matters of family.

The thing you never dared to fear.
But always there, and always here.
The thing outside that's looking in—
has always been, has always been.
(But since a face fills her house, too—
if it spares her, she might spare you.)

It's not contagious

A closet crammed with all the vaguest memories
of the life before this. Or—

it was a story full of characters, whose faces
were the faces of your friends, distorted.

Fun-house mirrors around every corner.
All the familiar places. The kitchen

is the one you used to cook in. The back
door opens into it, and a man you knew

a hundred years ago steps in, holding
a parcel of something you know you knew

the name of once. Vegetable, mineral—
something else? You step out of that door

and into the mouth of it. A cage
of wolves. They've been waiting.

Their panting is the smell of a sickroom.
But there's no illness. It's not contagious.

It's musical, and it sings to you. It uses
the nickname your father used to call you when

you were too little to be ashamed, in
a voice that isn't his but could have been.

CINDY2

A trash pile, an ash pit
full of girlhood memories. Memories
of girlhood returning
from the trash pits and ash piles in which
we burned them, and from your bedroom where we slept
in flannel pajamas, drank
from your mother's gin.

The dove went out, and it returned.

Silk bras and panties, and those ashes, and then
we got older, and still
I thought and thought
about you, until
finally

I guessed your password.

The swallow went out, and it also returned.

Now, after so much lust for your whole life, your
future and past which I also despised, like

those sounds your house
used to make after dark. Always a cello propped
up in a corner, although
no one ever played it. It
was the vibration, though, that
never ended. Your

stepfather called you, accidentally, over
and over by your mother's name. For

so long I'd think about your
cold wooden floor, your dresser drawers full of

voices, fluctuations, rubber bands, dried-up pens, Magic
Markers, and all the little pots of watercolors—dried up.
Crackled, colorless—even the little paint and makeup
brushes: those

bristles of a boar
in heat, or
headed for the slaughter, every hair stiffened, forever, even

the bright-pink plastic ribbons
and the glitter

and barrettes. There was forever some bottle or tube of
something expensive that would have made us beautiful, would
have made us smell like flowers, or flushed
our cheeks with shame, or turned our hair to silk, or set
our lips aflame (or so
the advertisements claimed) but the cap
was always off, lost, gone, so by then it had become
powder, the lotion. Dust, the balm. The violet-scented toilet water
was turned by time to paste, to mud. Now
all this
freedom. So much of it. This
access to these emails, these
bank accounts of yours: I could
become
you now—on
Facebook, on Twitter, on Pinterest.

The crow
went out, and the crow
did not come back.

(How
did I guess it? You
want to know? So
easily: because when

he called your mother's name
from the other side
of your bedroom door, you
answered him.) Now

I could be
anything you'll ever say or do
again, or ever did. This

treasure chest still
full of girlhood. What
to do with it? What to do with all this power
now that I

have all of it? Well

I'm expecting you to answer. I'm
waiting for your advice. *I sent out*
a dove
and it died.

No. If I seem
to have grown
suddenly quiet
it's only
because I'm willing to wait
a little longer: I've

got time to think about it, here
in your bedroom, at
your window, using your name.

The Pelican

for Doug Trevor

Its ancient eye, with which it swallows what it sees.
And its flight's complex machinery.
And a little girl's drawing of one of these. Imagine

a crayon in
a delicate hand. The hoarse

rasp of waves over rocks, turning
even the largest of them into sand. How

we might come upon certain creatures
again and again, always
where the air is thinnest, and brightest, which is
around the sharp edges
of our existences.

That bird's strange and unexpected gaze. I've

tried to picture her
(forgive me)—
your sister, the one I'll never meet, and never met.
I've felt, once or twice, that I could *wither*
her, I guess. Wherever she
was, and left, and then
the depths of your

love's spectacular wreckage, although

those birds, each
one in its dead fall, simply
disappears, leaves not even a single loose
stitch behind it on the surface of the water. Not

even a hint. But, surely, the return—its miracle
not less miraculous
for having been inevitable. This

one bearing your laughter this afternoon, almost
undamaged, it seems to me, suddenly, as

surprising as a little girl's drawing
of a pelican, forever. *Here*

she says. *I had*
to dive down deep and disappear for a long
time to find this
for you, but I did.

Red Mud Lake (3)

But what if I had claws, or long incisors, or
even a little knife? What if I threw
my arms around the neck of the beaten
horse in the street, as Nietzsche (or
was it Raskolnikov?)
once did?

Ah, you'd have to touch me then, wouldn't you?
You'd have to see what you'd done to me.

You, my mirage in a jar . . .
You, my tributary to the Amazon . . .
You, my sacred text held together without glue.

Without you, I fear nothing now, I fear.
Not even my own ugliness in a mirror.
You should love me more for this, I feel.
In fact, I feel certain of this.
I have grown more lovable without your love.
In fact, that you left me with nothing is also a fact.
So I have nothing left to lose:

Come closer. Even closer. I'm not afraid of you.

Gargoyle

The boat moves so slowly I've begun to wonder if, like the planet, it
      moves at all, or if
that's just another story I've come to believe because I told it.
This heat—

you'd recognize it. I know. Because once, a couple of
decades or so ago, you handed exactly this
kind of heat to me
in an unsealed envelope—

brief, and typed, on a sheet of onionskin with
a watermark in the middle. Also—

we lived in a hell like this together
for a while, like this, so hot we couldn't breathe. I won't bother to
      describe it—

I won't tell you anything about my life without you, either. You hate,
      or—
you hated

details then. Now—

Now I wouldn't know. But this child beside me on this boat—

this boy in the baseball cap, he's mine, but he's got nothing to do with
      us. He's
looking up into all this heat (it's—

as I already told you—so
hot today, such
burning on this boat) to see the gargoyles on the cathedral our
tour guide said we could see—

but I'm so nearsighted, as you know. And this boy, he's—

he's got nothing to do with us. He's with me. We float. So slowly. He
points and says, Look—
Mom! There they are. Looking down at us!

and maybe—I can't be sure, the sky's so bright, and I'm so
nearsighted, as you know, but—

I might see something like—

I might see something with a face made
of stone, or pestilence, or plague—

but *not contagious.*

Now we aren't even floating. I think we've—

No, we're just floating more
and more slowly. The others are taking photos. We've been
floating all along, so long that the thing I kept hidden inside me has
        crawled out—

These monsters. I believe in them. I believe
in the ghouls and ghosts and sinners and judges and persecutors of the
        innocent
I've been, which—

Look! he says again, pointing to them.
They're staring down at us, Mom. Can't you see?

I can't.
So hot, so bright. I close my eyes—

and then
I see, but it's a scene
from the New Testament. Maybe—

Jesus. He's bleeding and tending some sheep. He
carries a hook, but there are holes in his hands, and also his feet. Or—

maybe there are rusty nails still in them, and now—

we're floating faster. The thing's
on fire. The shadow of the shadow of the smoke is cast all over us. I
     want to go—

go backward, go home, but
we're going forward, growing older
and older. I'm so nearsighted, as you know, and now—

I'm forgetful also, now
more than I ever was, but I swear—

I saw it, and I never forgot it—

the expression on your face when I lied
straight to it. Look now, Mom—!

When I open my eyes I see
some stained-glass shards.
Someone assembled them
hundreds of years ago
into sacred light.

I want to be them
now. I want to go—

I want to be the woman who hands the tools to the assembler of those.
I want to go back to that and tell the truth—

I lied. And this time I want
my own face to reflect itself
in my own face, to blind

me, to see myself as you might—

as a woman on a boat, waving, stupidly, to the gargoyles
blurred by sun and smoke and glass—

all of it on fire, or sanctified, and—

Some of them have wings, he says, and some have horns, and some have
      ears and tails
and manes and crowns and all of them are hunched over, looking down
      at us, Mom—

and this time I allow you to be the disapproving one, the unforgiving
      one, the one
disgusted, or better yet, better than I deserve, and more than I should
      hope for—

the one so bored by this slow torture you only bother to notice how
much older I've grown. How much I suffer in this heat, how slowly
      the boat
I'm on, how—

slow, you'd think. How long ago. How old. And—

and I see something.
And she doesn't.
And that boy beside her must be her son. Just—

another kid who never wronged me. Despite his mother. Deserves
      to live.
Loves her, I suppose, and it's—

so hot, and I've watched generations of them pass below me. So
much trouble—

too much—

and you decide to let us go.

Red Mud Lake (4)

Your clothes are new.
The skirts, the dresses, the jeans, the sweaters. The shoes: all of them.
You've been wearing them forever, but you've never seen
the wardrobe of this stranger you were back then, until
this moment. You've never opened this closet
with this hand.
There are extra fingers on both of them. But you've forgotten how
many you should have. Then
you forget how to count. Arms
you never knew you had. You needed
extra arms so badly
when you were young, when you were a mother, but now
they're tangled, emptily, around one another. Your brain
can't contain so many, or so fast. You've got
a lesion, the doctor says. You
ask him how that word is spelled. But his
alphabet is someone else's. You
pretend to write it down on the piece of paper with the pen he gave you
but you can't find your right hand. Perhaps
you're left-handed? Have you always been? No, you tell him. This
isn't what the word is.
He looks at your piece of paper and then says, "Baby?"
Perhaps. Perhaps you wrote that down. And maybe you meant to do so. So
you say, "Yes." You say, "It's not a—"
"Lesion," he says. You say, "No," again. You say, "It's baby." You explain
to him that it was given to you by a stranger
the other day. She passed you in a parking lot and asked if you could hold
her baby. You said of course. You'd been a mother too. You wanted to help
her. You wanted her baby. You took it to the river, and—
"I'm sorry?" the doctor says—but he's not apologizing. He's asking you
a question. "No," you answer. "I didn't take it anywhere. I just stared
into its face, and it slipped through my eyes into my brain, and now
you're showing me a scan of that."

"Okay," he says. He takes out a pen and a pad of paper, the pad from which
he tore a single page for you. The pen
he gave you is now in his hand. "Can you tell me more about this?"
        he asks.
You could say no, but you want to tell him. Everyone should know. It will
comfort them. It will astonish them. You explain it's *like* a baby. You've
        had it
inside you since the day you were born.
"But it's a stranger's?"
Well, no. Not exactly. Unless I'm the stranger.

"Are you?" he asks.
I laugh.
"And the river?"
Oh, the river. The Volga maybe? The Thames perhaps? You're sorry but you
sincerely can't remember the name. This
was before the Tigris and Euphrates, of course, or you'd have gone straight
to the Fertile Crescent. Your options were limited. This
was the beginning of everything. "How
did you get to a foreign country before you were born?" he asks.
I compliment his question, but I feel exhausted by the task ahead of me,
        trying
to explain it to someone who should know
more about it than he does. I start with the lost coins in it, and the
        pendants.
A baby blanket, and how it floated along so pale pink or blue until it sank.
"With the baby?" he asks.
No, no. Not the baby, you tell him. You tell him how you either handed
        the baby
back to its mother or you left it somewhere mossy, cool, and very quiet
in the past, where it's growing, the doctor tells you, but not too fast.
Don't worry, you tell him. It's not a baby anymore. It's
grown so much older, so deeply and so slowly.

On the nature of things

Created, all of it, from the tiniest
of particles—all of it
from all, for nothing

can come from nothing
at all, and therefore cannot be removed
from all—

not fins nor wings nor claws nor paws, nor
especially my child's small

hand one afternoon, holding
my husband's hand
as they wandered to the edge
of a pier that wandered into
Lake Michigan, while I
stayed behind and watched them
from a blanket spread out on the sand.

The water, cold

and vast, and "Nature, so
plain and manifest."
The child, the man.
"Stuff is everlasting. Things abide."
But when

they turned from such a tender distance
to wave to me, they
were so mortal in appearance, I
lost all certainty

and gave it up—my
claim on them—and
it has not come back.

Lucretius, however, never wavered in his belief
that, having been created
once, we become "permanent
constituents of the universe," and

although Lucretius was driven
mad by a love potion, ill-prepared and given
to him by his wife, Lucilla, he sat down
every morning, nonetheless, every morning
at a table to write
of the origin, of
the structure, of the destiny of
our eternalness

in Latin verse, while

Lucilla watched him, jealous
even of a poem, reading
each of his words as it
was being written, and

arguing against the creatures, the winds, the
little particles he called atoms, as if

even the stones, and the cups, the dogs
at the door, the flies
on the meat
existed in a never-ending universe! As if

it could just go on like this! Until

Lucretius could stand it no longer, and, with-
out having ended his poem, he
ended his life, putting

an end to the end of the end of all this.

Everyone together at the lake

At home there was a moth trapped alone in the refrigerator
in the cold, which is the dark, which that
day at the lake we ignored because—

Look!
Look at that sail! Look at that sail
on that sailboat! It's
like an envelope. It floats
away with our, all of—

Look. I found

these in the attic: some ruined photographs.

Some ruined photographs of some
other family's strangers gathered at a lake, but they
were better at this than we were. They woke up
early every morning to dance while we
waited in the cold of that: that colder

terror of the colder places. How can you

not remember that? You
were there just like the rest of us.
Here's the proof of it in my hand.
I found it ruined in the attic.

All of us at the lake.
The hundreds, the billions
of the many every morning. Oh

who knew, who's always known? Look at the sail
on that boat. Would you look at that?—who
would ever have known?—would you look at the sail on the lake
of that boat?

If, say—you?
If, say—you?
If I admit that you
had the colder
terror that afternoon? At

home, that moth trapped
in the cold
with a chalice, knowing

and knowing—
(and look: some
more ruined photographs! I
found them in the attic! All of us. And me and you.
Who knew? Who would you have guessed?)

If I said—you?

If I said—I know you knew?
If I said, *you were the one,* would
you look then?
Look anyway, and tell me
whether or not you saw it, and whether
or not it was sailing in our direction
or in someone else's.
Was it

slicing toward the horizon
or toward the shore?
If you were trapped alone—
If I said *you?*
Would you have guessed
if I said that?

If I told you the truth that we both know
you already knew, what then?

There we were with our backs to it
while you snapped a photo of it, looking
straight at it, straight past all of us
smiling together
at the lake
that day
at you
taking a photograph
while a sail sliced through
the blue.
Look.

Look at that.

And then
look away. Never
look back.

Paint

Here we are with the whole palette, and the cans and the brushes and
    trays. We have
Amsterdam here—yes, the blue that makes you think of April, of canals,
    but also of Anne

Frank, her diary in that attic, which is the color of desperate joy snatched
    from a girl's
throat before it could be had. Muslin, maybe. Shroud. Or Moss. You
    wanted

Raisin Torte instead. I wanted Mayonnaise. Raccoon Fur. I wanted even
    layers of the shade
they painted my grandmother's nervous breakdown and my mother's last
    cancer-ravaged

rage. Hospital, USA. Some Midwestern state, like Wisconsin. Remember?
    The room
with the tub with those brass knobs? How drunk we got with your college
    buddy (Joe?)

dead a couple decades now? *That's* the color I wanted to sleep with every
    night, to be surrounded
by it, but also to hold it in my arms, especially after you're gone. But it's
    too late to argue anymore

about this now. The painters are here and want to know what color we
    decided on.
"*Fatigue,*" I whisper to you: "Or *Resignation.*" Or something in between.
Like *Lassitude. Prostration.* But you

won't do it, of course. They're just college guys, wearing backward
    baseball caps. They smell
like weed. They want the money, and they've only come to smile at us
    because we have the walls and what they need.

I hear

They could be semis on the freeway, or locusts   eating   eating   or it
    could be laughter from across the street.

I'd listen, but there's a man in the warehouse marching around with
    industrial-sized fans. He's

swearing about a cigarette. He shouts, "No one gives a fuck! Shut up!"
    to someone who doesn't seem to be there or to be talking.

But I heard him, too, myself, and
behind him I heard the cemeteries flying
by on the freeway—or, not cemeteries: semis. And

locusts. My God, all these transparent children and their invisible
    laughter. Their

laughter, being, as laughter is, their teeth and lungs, electrified.

Honey? Where's the flashlight? Where's the butcher knife? Did you
    drive my Jeep
somewhere and leave it?

I don't know. My wallet? Have you seen it?
Did you see
my baby? Did you see
any baby?

I heard a woman shout this once
and she never stopped shouting it
until my whole torso, like a gong, trembled
all of me. Or

like an arrow
in my eye, or
with a song that sunlight might pour all over the summer when you
can't find your child. No. That

could be no song.
But if it wasn't a song and wasn't some
ravenous, irrational insect in the mind, what
could it have been except the song I heard until I died?

Prayer

The windshield's dirty, the squirter stuff's all gone, so
we drive on together into a sun-gray pane of grime
and dust. My son

puts the passenger seat back as far as it will go, closes
his eyes. I crack my window open for a bit
of fresher air. It's so

incredibly fresh out there.

Rain, over.
Puddles left
in ditches. Black mirrors with our passing

reflected in them, I suppose, but I'd
have to pull over and kneel down at the side
of the road to know.

The day ahead—

for this, the radio
doesn't need to be played.
The house we used to live in

still exists
in a snapshot, in which
it yellows in another family's scrapbook.

And a man on a bicycle
rides beside us
for a long time, very swiftly, until finally

he can't keep up—

but before he slips
behind us, he salutes us
with his left hand—

a reminder:

that every single second—
that every prisoner on death row—
that every name on every tombstone—

that everywhere we go—
that every day, like
this one, will
be like every other, having never

been never ending. So
thank you. And, oh—I
almost forgot to say: amen.

ACKNOWLEDGMENTS

Some of these poems appeared in the following:

The Academy of American Poets Poem-a-Day: "Prayer," "The time machine"

The Adroit Journal: "No elegy"

The American Journal of Poetry: "CINDY2," "Everyone together at the lake," "Red Mud Lake (4)"

American Literary Review: "A Girl's Guide to Color," "The Pelican"

Conduit: "It's not contagious," "True Crime (1)"

The Georgia Review: "Gargoyle," "When a bolt of lightning falls in love"

Ghost Town: "My first mistress"

Gulf Coast: "Suffering song"

Kenyon Review: "For the return of the bee," "On the nature of things"

Michigan Quarterly Review: "Secrets," "True Crime (1)"

On the Seawall: "The house sitter"

Plume Poetry 7 anthology: "Eleven girls"

Poetry: "The eavesdropper," "Talisman"

Rattle: "The odyssey"

The Yale Review: "A doll's house"

"An evil meal," "Rescue Annie," and "Two gardens" were first published in the chapbook *The Time Machine* by Willow Springs Books. Thank you to Taylor D. Waring, Kari Rueckert, Cassandra Bruner, Catie Feldman, Jordan Dunn, and Thomas Doyle, and to the Acme Poem Company Surrealist Poetry Series, for publishing these and other poems.

I am indebted forever to my editor, Michael Wiegers, and to all who've offered me so much help and support at Copper Canyon Press, especially John Pierce, Jessica Roeder, Laura Buccieri, and Phil Kovacevich.

I am eternally grateful to the Residential College at the University of Michigan and to my colleagues there, some of whom were also my teachers—particularly Laura Thomas, Cindy Sowers, Warren Hecht, Ken Mikolowski, and Van Jordan—and also to my inspiring Residential College students.

About the Author

Laura Kasischke has previously published eleven collections of poetry and eleven works of fiction. She was the recipient of the National Book Critics Circle Award for Poetry in 2011. She has also received the Rilke Award for Poetry, a Guggenheim Fellowship, and France's Prix Elle for the best novel of the year. She teaches at the University of Michigan and lives in Chelsea, Michigan.

Lannan Literary Selections

For two decades Lannan Foundation has supported the publication and distribution of exceptional literary works. Copper Canyon Press gratefully acknowledges their support.

LANNAN LITERARY SELECTIONS 2021

Shangyang Fang, *Burying the Mountain*

June Jordan, *The Essential June Jordan*

Laura Kasischke, *Lightning Falls in Love*

Arthur Sze, *The Glass Constellation: New and Collected Poems*

Fernando Valverde (translated by Carolyn Forché), *America*

RECENT LANNAN LITERARY SELECTIONS FROM COPPER CANYON PRESS

Mark Bibbins, *13th Balloon*

Sherwin Bitsui, *Dissolve*

Jericho Brown, *The Tradition*

Victoria Chang, *Obit*

Leila Chatti, *Deluge*

John Freeman, *Maps*

Jenny George, *The Dream of Reason*

Deborah Landau, *Soft Targets*

Rachel McKibbens, *blud*

Philip Metres, *Shrapnel Maps*

Aimee Nezhukumatathil, *Oceanic*

Camille Rankine, *Incorrect Merciful Impulses*

Paisley Rekdal, *Nightingale*

Natalie Scenters-Zapico, *Lima :: Limón*

Natalie Shapero, *Popular Longing*

Frank Stanford, *What About This: Collected Poems of Frank Stanford*

C.D. Wright, *Casting Deep Shade*

Matthew Zapruder, *Father's Day*

Poetry is vital to language and living. Since 1972, Copper Canyon Press has published extraordinary poetry from around the world to engage the imaginations and intellects of readers, writers, booksellers, librarians, teachers, students, and donors.

Copper Canyon Press gratefully acknowledges the kindness, patronage, and generous support of Jean Marie Lee, whose love and passionate appreciation of poetry has provided an everlasting benefit to our publishing program.

WE ARE GRATEFUL FOR THE MAJOR SUPPORT PROVIDED BY:

THE PAUL G. ALLEN
FAMILY FOUNDATION

CULTURE

Lannan

OFFICE OF ARTS & CULTURE
SEATTLE

WASHINGTON STATE
ARTS COMMISSION

TO LEARN MORE ABOUT UNDERWRITING
COPPER CANYON PRESS TITLES,
PLEASE CALL 360-385-4925 EXT. 103

WE ARE GRATEFUL FOR THE MAJOR SUPPORT PROVIDED BY:

Anonymous

Jill Baker and Jeffrey Bishop

Anne and Geoffrey Barker

In honor of Ida Bauer, Betsy
Gifford, and Beverly Sachar

Donna and Matthew Bellew

Will Blythe

John Branch

Diana Broze

John R. Cahill

Sarah Cavanaugh

The Beatrice R. and Joseph A.
Coleman Foundation

The Currie Family Fund

Stephanie Ellis-Smith and Douglas
Smith

Austin Evans

Saramel Evans

Mimi Gardner Gates

Gull Industries Inc. on behalf of
William True

The Trust of Warren A. Gummow

William R. Hearst, III

Carolyn and Robert Hedin

Bruce Kahn

Phil Kovacevich and Eric Wechsler

Lakeside Industries Inc. on behalf
of Jeanne Marie Lee

Maureen Lee and Mark Busto

Peter Lewis and Johnna Turiano

Ellie Mathews and Carl Youngmann
as The North Press

Larry Mawby and Lois Bahle

Hank and Liesel Meijer

Jack Nicholson

Gregg Orr

Petunia Charitable Fund and
adviser Elizabeth Hebert

Suzanne Rapp and Mark Hamilton

Adam and Lynn Rauch

Emily and Dan Raymond

Joseph C. Roberts

Jill and Bill Ruckelshaus

Cynthia Sears

Kim and Jeff Seely

Joan F. Woods

Barbara and Charles Wright

Caleb Young as C. Young Creative

The dedicated interns and
faithful volunteers of
Copper Canyon Press

The Chinese character for poetry is made up of two parts:
"word" and "temple." It also serves as pressmark for
Copper Canyon Press.

The poems are set in Adobe Garamond Pro.
Book design and composition by Phil Kovacevich.